Benedikt Link

Primed to cheat

Stealing your co-worker's idea to stay in business

Anchor Compact

Link, Benedikt: Primed to cheat. Stealing your co-worker's idea to stay in business.
Hamburg, Anchor Academic Publishing 2013

Buch-ISBN: 978-3-95489-162-7
PDF-eBook-ISBN: 978-3-95489-662-2
Druck/Herstellung: Anchor Academic Publishing, Hamburg, 2013

Bibliografische Information der Deutschen Nationalbibliothek:
Die Deutsche Nationalbibliothek verzeichnet diese Publikation in der Deutschen
Nationalbibliografie; detaillierte bibliografische Daten sind im Internet über
http://dnb.d-nb.de abrufbar.

All rights reserved. This publication may not be reproduced, stored in a retrieval system
or transmitted, in any form or by any means, electronic, mechanical, photocopying,
recording or otherwise, without the prior permission of the publishers.

Das Werk einschließlich aller seiner Teile ist urheberrechtlich geschützt. Jede Verwertung
außerhalb der Grenzen des Urheberrechtsgesetzes ist ohne Zustimmung des Verlages
unzulässig und strafbar. Dies gilt insbesondere für Vervielfältigungen, Übersetzungen,
Mikroverfilmungen und die Einspeicherung und Bearbeitung in elektronischen Systemen.

Die Wiedergabe von Gebrauchsnamen, Handelsnamen, Warenbezeichnungen usw. in
diesem Werk berechtigt auch ohne besondere Kennzeichnung nicht zu der Annahme,
dass solche Namen im Sinne der Warenzeichen- und Markenschutz-Gesetzgebung als frei
zu betrachten wären und daher von jedermann benutzt werden dürften.

Die Informationen in diesem Werk wurden mit Sorgfalt erarbeitet. Dennoch können
Fehler nicht vollständig ausgeschlossen werden und der Diplomica Verlag, die Autoren
oder Übersetzer übernehmen keine juristische Verantwortung oder irgendeine Haftung
für evtl. verbliebene fehlerhafte Angaben und deren Folgen.

Alle Rechte vorbehalten

© Anchor Academic Publishing, Imprint der Diplomica Verlag GmbH
Hermannstal 119k, 22119 Hamburg
http://www.diplomica-verlag.de, Hamburg 2013
Printed in Germany

Acknowledgement

I would like to thank my wife Thea for her relentless emotional support and Dr Jonathan E. Booth for providing me with this great learning experience.

Abstract

This study aims to show that situational cues like semantic primes are able to influence a participant's decision-making in the context of taking credit for someone else's idea at the workplace. In a laboratory experiment either a competitive, cooperative or neutral environment was simulated by using subliminal priming techniques. Participants were then exposed to a hypothetical scenario in which they were urged – due to their heavy workload – to take credit for a colleague's idea. In particular, the study examined four constructs: the participants' willingness to take credit for this idea without and with escalating consequences for not choosing to do it, the perceived ethical costs related to that action and the perception of others mindsets. It was expected that participants in the competitive condition would be more willing to take credit for the colleague's idea and perceive less ethical costs than in the neutral condition and vice versa for the participants in the cooperative condition. Additionally, the study expected the participants to perceive the mindset of a random other in the same situation to be similar to their own mindset. Furthermore, qualitative data was collected to explore the decision-making process in such a situation. The results showed that situational cues did not significantly influence the individual decision-making in this particular context. However, several unexpected findings about the relationships between the tested constructs deliver valuable implications for future research on the topic of taking credit for other people's ideas. In addition, the findings from the qualitative analysis suggest that future studies have to differentiate between ethical and utilitarian considerations to gain further insights into the individual decision-making process.

Table of Contents

1. INTRODUCTION 1

2. THEORY AND HYPOTHESES 3
   2.1 The role of subliminal priming 3
   2.2 Willingness to take credit without and with escalating severity of consequences ... 4
   2.3 Perceived ethical costs 7
   2.4 Perception of others' mindset 8

3. METHODOLOGY 10

4. RESULTS 15
   4.1 Quantitative results 15
   4.2 Qualitative results 18

5. DISCUSSION 20

6. LIMITATIONS 24

7. CONCLUSION AND IMPLICATIONS 26

APPENDIX 28
REFERENCES 48

1. Introduction

In his book "The rise of the knowledge worker" James Cortada (1998) describes the change in industrialized and increasingly computerized countries: More and more workers are required not to manufacture new goods anymore, but to provide knowledge and information to those who still do. In fact, with the manufacturing industries declining and the shift to service and knowledge sectors in developed countries, the importance of generating new ideas and innovation has risen over the last decades (Schettkat/Yocarini 2003).

With increasing importance of ideas, they more and more pose a competitive advantage for workers who have ideas over those who don't. Following this thought, Wang and Noe (2010: 124) found in the literature about knowledge sharing that ideas can act as positive factors in one's performance evaluation and thus in promotions, bonuses and other forms of personal gains. They also mention that employees in possession of valuable ideas will tend to guard them and thus keep their status as an expert in a particular area. As with any other resource, individuals who are in need of a valuable idea, but are not able to obtain it for whatever reason, might be tempted to illegally take credit for an idea of another person. A popular example for this poses the former German Minister of Defence, Karl-Theodor zu Guttenberg, who was recently stripped of doctorate due to plagiarism. He justified the substantial copying with his heavy workload as member of the German parliament while raising his two daughters (Pidd 2011).

The present study is primary concerned with the temptation to take credit for a colleague's idea when unable to cope with one's own job demands in competitive or in cooperative work environments. Thereby, it is important to clearly distinguish ideas from intellectual property. Intellectual property rights can only be claimed by the author of an idea if the respective idea has taken form in some way, e.g. as a drawing or a picture of an invention (patent, trade mark), a physical appearance (design) or a written document (copyright) that is then officially registered (Intellectual Property Office 2007). Thus, in contrast to intellectual property, it remains debatable if it is theft to take credit for an idea that was merely verbally mentioned by someone else, especially if that person is working within the same company.

So far, past research has mainly focused on the effects of competitive work environment on the willingness of workers to share information with each other (e.g. Steinel et al. 2010 ; Carpenter/Seki 2006 ; Burks et al. 2005 ; Drago/Garvey 1998). Actively taking credit for someone else's ideas has rather been neglected. The only relevant study about taking credit for someone else's idea at the workplace that could be identified in preparation of the present study was authored by *OfficeTeam*, a staffing specialist company (Krumrie 2010). This study included telephone interviews of 444 workers and found that 29 % had experienced a coworker taking credit for one of their ideas. However, the survey didn't ask if any of the interviewed persons ever took credit for someone else's idea and about their motivations to do so.

The present research seeks to fill this gap by pursuing two goals. The first goal is to show that situational influences can activate competitively or cooperatively processing mindsets that are strong enough to alter an individual's decision to take credit for a colleague's idea regardless one's personality or personal disposition. In particular, four aspects are examined: the willingness of an individual to take credit for someone else's idea without or with escalating severity of anticipated consequences for not taking credit, the individual's ethical considerations about this action and the individual's perception of the mindsets of others. The situational influences in form of either a competitive or cooperative environment will be thereby artificially created by using subliminal priming techniques in an artificial laboratory experiment. The second goal is to develop a comprehensive basis for future research in the field of stealing ideas by asking questions about why it would be right or wrong to take credit for someone else's ideas. This shall enhance our understanding of the underlying reasoning in the participants' decision-making process.

2. Theory and Hypotheses

2.1 The role of subliminal priming

The method of subliminal priming was used in this study to artificially produce either a competitive or cooperative environment that affects the participants' behaviour with situational cues. *Subliminal* in this context means – as opposed to *supraliminal* – that primes affect individuals below their threshold of cognitive awareness (Bargh/Pietromonaco 1982).

In the literature about social cognition *primes* represent subtle manipulations that activate certain mentally represented concepts via associative links (Bargh et al. 1996, Dijksterhuis et al. 1998). Research has shown that priming can alter a person's perceptions of others (e.g. Herr 1986), which then influence behavioural responses to or processing of a certain piece of information. In Herr's study (1986), participants were primed with the concept of hostility, which made them perceiving others more hostile towards them and therefore reduced the level of cooperation. Notably, these studies focused merely on the participants' perceptions of other actors with a mediating effect on behavioural responses.

Other studies have shown that those activated concepts can directly trigger related behavioural responses, even if only weak cues were used to *prime* the participants in an experiment (e.g. Srull&Wyer 1979 ; Bargh et al. 2001 ; Maxwell et al. 1999 ; Good 1973). A study by Bargh et al. (1996) depicts the impact of such cues: merely exposing participants to an elderly stereotype induced them to walk down a hallway slower than those in the neutral control group did. In another study, Kay & Ross (2003) sought to show that situational constructs and norms have a mediating role on behaviour. They argued that such situational cues can greatly predict social behaviour. Their findings demonstrated that priming persons either exposed to competitive or cooperative cues had a significant effect on the persons' subsequent behavioural intentions. The present study seeks to build on these findings by showing that competitive and cooperative cues can also influence behavioural perceptions and intentions towards stealing someone else's ideas.

It has to be noted that such manipulations are expected to function best in ambiguous or novel situations. Extending Fiske and Taylor's assumption that people try to minimize cognitive resources by established scripts about how to deal with familiar situations, Kay et al. (2004: 84) showed in a study about priming with physical objects that people's decisions and perceptions in ambiguous or unfamiliar situations tend to rely on external (environmental) cues. Consequently, participants in the present study's experiment were confronted with a hypothetical situation that was kept as ambiguous as possible.

2.2 Willingness to take credit without and with escalating severity of consequences

In the literature about the *dark side* of the organisation – involving all intentional behaviour by an entity in an organization with negative consequences for another entity (Griffin/O'Leary-Kelly 2004) – two perspectives are generally considered: the bad individual per se and the bad organisation with negative influence on the individual.

Evidence exists that there are certain personality traits, which can be responsible for dark side behaviour such as taking credit for someone else's idea. Blickle and Schlegel (2006) found e.g. in their study among 150 managers and convicted 76 *white-collar* felons that certain traits are likely to be responsible for engaging in *white-collar crime*: higher levels of hedonism and narcissistic personality disorder and lower levels of behavioural self-control and conscientiousness indicated a higher likeliness to commit offences.

However, there is reason to assume that an individual's surroundings significantly affect his or her intentions and behaviour regardless the individual's personal disposition. There is e.g. empirical evidence that an individual's level of *dark side* behaviour is in fact influenced by the overall level of this behaviour in his or her work group. In a study by Robinson and O'Leary-Kelly (1998) perceived antisocial group behaviour (such as stealing or saying something bad about a colleague) was positively related to each group member's antisocial behaviour.

The mere working conditions also present a viable influence: Employees who perceive that their job demands exceed their coping resources (one's own effort to succeed in one's job) feel overwhelmed (Demerouti et al. 2001). Agnew's *general strain* theory (1992, in Langton/Piquero 2007: 2) assumes that the failure to achieve a goal or to meet job demands is likely to result in mental strain. Thus, employees will be urged to look for ways to regain control over the work environment. The decision or rather the justification which way is the right to choose is thereby also likely to be influenced by the employees' environment itself. *Social information processing* theory (Salancik/Pfeffer 1978: 224) suggests that an individual develops attitudes and socially acceptable rationalisations based on the available social information. Next to the consequences of own past choices this information is provided by other employees and the organisation itself, i.e. the social environment of the individual. The following paragraphs consider two kind of environments and their expected effect on an individual under pressure, which is relevant for this study: a competitive and a cooperative environment.

Labour economists have addressed in the past how employees under pressure will behave in a competitive work environment (Lazear 1989, Lazear/Gibbs 2009, Chen 2003, Green/Stokey 1983). In a so-called "tournament" (Lazear/Gibbs 2009: 298) a firm rewards or promotes its employees for their performance. The competitive factor derives from a relative performance measurement rather than from an absolute standard: it does not primarily matter if an employee reaches a certain performance, but it does matter if he or she is doing better than her colleagues (Lazear/Gibbs 2009). This implies two principles. First, competition motivates employees to increase their effort in order to win (Lazear/Rosen 1981). Second, it can decrease cooperation among them and push them to engage in sabotaging their colleagues (Lazear 1989). Such "predatory behaviour" (Lazear 1989: 562) can include stealing information from them to make up for one's – insufficient – effort. This paragraph explained how workers react in a environment with high pressure from competition. The next paragraph will go further into detail about why they react that way.

This does not necessarily imply the intention to harm the co-worker who is sabotaged, i.e. is ripped of his or her idea, but primary to secure one's survival at the workplace (Rosenfeld et al. 1995). As found in a study by Harrell-Cook et al. (1999), this kind of behaviour serves as a coping mechanism for one's own incompetence. Such a form of impression management is described by Bratton and Kacmar and involves next to blaming, discrediting, intimidation and negative projection also "taking credit for someone else's work" (2004: 296). They further explain that this harmful form of impression management is triggered by contextual variables such as uncertainty that partially arises when one's own competence doesn't seem enough to succeed (Bratton/Kacmar 2004).

In contrast to a competitive environment, a cooperative environment, in which individual performance evaluation is based on group performance or on absolute standards, has a rather opposite effect. A study, conducted by Carpenter and Seki (2006) in a Japanese fishing community shows that the nature of a respective work environment has distinct outcomes on an individual's attitude. Their findings are that the fishermen who are not organized in collaborative groups faced a highly competitive environment. They engaged in less cooperation than the fish traders and the administrative staff of the community, who faced a less competitive work environment. This study demonstrated how the work environment and job demands lead to different outcomes on individuals who even shared a common background after all: all workplaces were situated in the same community (Carpenter/Seki 2006).

Notably, the level of collaboration is positively related to the level of cohesiveness in a group of employees (Bakker et al. 2006; Sawng et al 2006). The level of group cohesiveness indicates the level of mutual trust and assurance that none of them will take advantage of the other members and also to what extent they comply to shared norms and goals (Lauring/Selmer 2010).

If faced by a heavy workload or similar threats, individuals in a competitive environment might therefore be less inclined to collaborate and instead engage in taking credit for a colleague's idea. In contrast, individuals in a cooperative environment might be eager to uphold the level of collaboration and resist the urge to take credit. Based on these thoughts, it can be predicted that:

Hypothesis 1: When unable to cope with their job demands, individuals in the competitive priming condition are more willing and individuals in the cooperative priming condition are less willing to take credit for someone else's idea than individuals in the neutral condition are.

Following the same rationale, it can also be assumed that the willingness to take credit for someone else's idea is likely to increase if the anticipated consequences for not doing it cause increasing costs to the individual, like e.g. getting a worse performance appraisal or being dismissed. In a study about an individual's commitment to engaging in software piracy, i.e. stealing intellectual property, Glass and Wood (1996) found that the willingness to commit piracy is positively correlated with the likelihood of obtaining favourable outcomes in return. Despite the initially mentioned distinction between ideas and intellectual property, it seems reasonable to assume that the motivation to engage in such behaviour is similar in the case of stealing ideas: The negative consequences pose an additional source of strain to the employee that he or she will try to minimize in order to obtain a more favourable outcome:

Hypothesis 2: When unable to cope with their job demands, individuals in the competitive priming condition are more willing and individuals in the cooperative priming condition are less willing to take credit for someone else's idea with escalating severity of anticipated consequences for not taking credit for the idea than individuals in the neutral condition.

2.3 Perceived ethical costs

The issue with claiming intellectual property rights for an idea was initially mentioned in the introduction. One could assume that taking credit for someone else's idea is stealing and therefore violates legal or societal norms, i.e. causes ethical costs to the individual and society as a whole. Still, stealing always entails by definition a violation of another person's rights of ownership in a fundamental way (Green 2007). With ownership and ideas being not a clear-cut relationship, taking credit for someone else's idea allows a lot of subjectivity in perceiving ethical costs associated with that action, especially if one takes into account the culturally and historically conditioned mental model of ethical behaviour of an individual (Chen/Choi 2005). Individuals might simply fail to recognize taking credit for someone else's idea as a moral issue (Glass/Wood 1996). Indeed, studies have shown that ethical decision-making is a highly complex process that is subject to a variety of personal dispositions. Various studies show that ethical reasoning is influenced e.g. by age, work experience, gender and cultural heritage (Chiu/Spindel 2009).

However, other authors mention that the decision-making process is influenced by an individual's "contextual rationality" (Guy 1990: 34), i.e. the generation and selection of feasible alternatives is embedded in the context. In fact, Bekkers (2004) expects in a study about the stability of individual social value orientations, which also entail personal competitive and cooperative dispositions, that situational cues like primes have been responsible for the low stability of social value orientations in the study's experiment.

Guy (1990) describes the ethical decision-making process in four stages. In the first stage, the problem and the desired outcomes in all relevant dimensions are determined. Stage two involves an evaluation which values might be affected in the process. In step three, an individual identifies all feasible alternatives considering all dimensions of the problem. Additionally, it is evaluated which values would be maximised or minimised by choosing a respective alternative. In the final step, the individual chooses the alternative, which maximises the value that is the most important to the individual and still solves the problem. The whole process is highly subjective and the weighting to what extent which values are affected by an alternative depends largely on the individual.

Assuming that situational cues influence the individual's ethical decision-making, those who are exposed to competition primes might consider pro-social values (e.g. mutual trust in one's team) as less important than pro-self values (e.g. success in one's career) and vice versa for participants in a cooperative priming condition. For competitively primed individuals the decision to take credit for someone else's idea would incur a minor, if any, norm violation, i.e. negligible ethical costs. As Sims (2003) notes that people who face competition may focus only on winning and accept behaving unethically as necessary mean toward one's own end. Considering that individuals in a cooperative environment are likely to try to maintain a high level of collaboration – as mentioned above – taking credit for someone else's idea would pose a severe norm violation. This would cause the individual to perceive higher ethical costs despite the inability to cope with one's job demands.

Hypothesis 3: When unable to cope with their job demands, individuals in the competitive priming condition perceive less ethical costs and individuals in the cooperative priming condition perceive more ethical costs in taking credit for someone else's idea than individuals in the neutral condition.

Due to the complexity of the ethical decision-making process, the present study also explores why an individual would think that taking credit for someone else's idea is the right or not the right thing to do and also what that individual thinks what someone else in the same situation would consider as the right or wrong thing to do. Therefore, participants in the present study were asked four open-ended questions. These will be explained in more detail in the methodology section of this study.

2.4 Perception of others' mindset
As outlined above in the section about subliminal priming, there is reason to assume that priming effects alter an individual's perception about how other people think. Therefore, this study also seeks to confirm that individuals in a competitive or cooperative priming condition would perceive another person in the same situation – without any further information about this person – to have a similar competitive or cooperative mindset. Theoretically and empirically, this is widely supported by authors about social cognition (e.g. Tversky/Kahneman 1974). The basic thought is that once a certain concept becomes activated, i.e. more accessi-

ble, it is more likely that an individual uses this concept in the assessment of others (Srull/Wyer 1979). Tversky and Kahneman named this a "judgemental heuristic" (1974: 1127) or shortcut that allows an individual to reduce information overload or – in the case of an ambiguous person or situation – information scarcity before rendering a judgment about another person's mindset or attitude. The individual uses the recently activated concept because it comes more easily to his or her mind.

Multiple studies have examined this phenomenon. In an experiment by Higgins et al. (1997) subjects were asked to describe another person in a hypothetical situation subsequently to priming activities. The researchers found that the subjects in the priming condition used words to describe the person's personality traits that were similar to the words that have been used to prime the subjects. In another study, Hertel and Kerr (2001) found that priming the concept *loyalty* made their participants more likely to believe that the other participants in the same group would expect loyalty as well. Notably, the target which individuals perceive to have a similar mindset do not have to be the person or group the individuals are competing against or collaborating with (Stapel/Koomen 2005).

Based on these thoughts, the present study expects:

Hypothesis 4: Individuals in the competitive priming condition perceive others' mindsets to be more competitive and individuals in the cooperative priming condition perceive others' mindsets to be more cooperative than individuals in the neutral condition do.

3. Methodology

Participants and design. The participants were 64 postgraduate and PhD students recruited at the London School of Economics and Political Science. 22 of them were native English speakers, 34 of them were female. The design of the experiment was between-groups with the three priming conditions as independent variables (competition vs neutral vs cooperation). The dependent variables were the participant's *Willingness to take credit*, *Willingness to take credit with escalating severity of consequences* for not choosing to take credit for the idea, the *Perceived ethical costs* in connection with the decision to take credit and the *Perception of others' mindset*.

Procedure and materials. Participants came to a laboratory at the university in varying numbers and were welcomed by a male experimenter. They were told that they would participate individually in three unrelated activities that would deal with word processing skills and decision-making in a specific work situation. After the introduction, they were brought into the main room with 20 individual booths and were told to choose a booth at their own convenience. Every booth had been outfitted with an envelope containing the three activities prior to the participants entering the room. That way each participant was blindly assigned to one condition (competition, cooperation or neutral). While the participants were working on the activities, they were not able to see each other. The three activities included (1) two word processing tasks representing the priming procedure, (2) the scenario and related questions (unless noted otherwise, all items were on a 7-point Likert response format) and (3) a manipulation check item, items for the Core Self Evaluation (CSE) score (Judge et al. 2003) and the Altruism score (on a 5-point Likert response format) (Penner et al. 2005) and demographic information (control variables) and funnel debriefing questions. After participants completed all activities, they individually submitted the envelope at the experimenter's desk, were handed their reward and were thanked for their participation. On average, it took the participants 40 minutes to complete all three activities. Each participant was rewarded with a chocolate bar plus the chance to win a 50 £ voucher.

Priming procedure. In the first activity, participants were confronted with two word-processing tasks, which were used as a subliminal priming technique. The first task was a word search puzzle as used in a study by Kleiman and Hassin (2001) and required the participant to find and mark words (provided in a list below) in a square of letters. In the competition and cooperation group, 6 of the 12 words in this list were prime words. In the competition group participants were confronted with words like battle, compete and rivalry, whereas in the cooperation group participants were exposed to words like commune, cooperation and group. In the neutral group words for objects were used (e.g. carpet, chair, picture) to avoid any undesired priming effects.

In the second priming task, participants were asked to rearrange 24 scrambled sentences that were used in studies by Kay and Ross (2003) and Smeesters et al. (2003). 16 of those sentences contained prime words similar to the words from the first task. All tasks used in activity 1 were identical to tasks that have been used in prior studies and proven to have a significant priming effect. Those prime words were included to produce a semantic and subliminal priming effect (Marslen-Wilson et al. 1994).

In activity 3, participants were asked to indicate on a 7-point Likert response format whether they feel rather competitive or cooperative. This item was included to provide a manipulation check to control for the effectiveness of the prime words.

Measuring the constructs. Activity 2 included a fictional scenario in which the participant takes on the role of an employee that is urged by his/her boss to have developed an idea by the end of the week for an important marketing campaign. Every employee on this team has to develop an individual idea for the meeting. Due to his/her heavy workload, this employee is not able to produce an idea. Coincidentally, he/she overhears a colleague called Sam talking on the phone about a very good idea for the marketing campaign. On the next team meeting, the employee has the chance to take credit for his/her colleague's idea. Based on this scenario, the participants then answered a questionnaire containing 26 items related to the four different constructs.

To test Hypothesis 1, five questions about the participants' basic willingness to take credit for the colleague's idea, whether they would hesitate or have doubts to do so and how often they would think about it prior to the team meeting. For comparative reasons, another item, which asked participants about the percentaged chance with that he or she would take credit for the colleague's idea, was included using a continuous scale from 1 to a 100 percent.

For Hypothesis 3, participants were then asked whether they agree with statements arguing that e.g. taking credit for the colleague's idea would be the right decision and therefore would not cause any harm to anyone. The items were created by drawing on literature about ethical decision-making (Guy 1990). In addition, two open-ended items gave the participants the possibility to explain:

> *Can you think of any other arguments why it would be right to take credit for Sam's idea?*
>
> *Can you think of any other arguments why it would NOT be right to take credit for Sam's idea?*

Subsequently, participants were confronted with four items that asked once again about their willingness to take credit for this idea, but this time in anticipation of exacerbating consequences (including receiving a bad performance appraisal, not being promoted, being demoted and being fired) (Hypothesis 2), if the participant decided not to take credit and didn't have an idea during the team meeting.

To measure the perception of other's mindset (Hypothesis 4), the participants were asked to imagine that not they, but another random teammate would overhear the colleague's phone call and could take credit for this idea during the next team meeting. No additional information about this other teammate was provided to keep it as ambiguous as possible. The five items for this scale included aspects of the previous three scales with the difference that the participants had to indicate the expected behaviour of that teammate in the same context.

Furthermore, the participants were asked to further explain in two open-ended questions:

> *Why do you believe that your teammate would think that taking credit for Sam's idea is the right thing to do?*
>
> *Why do you believe that your teammate would think that taking credit for Sam's idea is NOT the right thing to do?*

For a more reliable and consistent measurement of the four constructs, scales for each of the constructs were developed based on inter-item correlations. This was necessary because no other study in which similar measures had already been used could be found prior to this study. In the first step of the data analysis, items were therefore grouped in varying combinations in order to reach a preferably high internal consistency. As measure, Cronbach's ☐ (on standardized items) was used. This measure reflects how well each included item correlates with the sum of the other items in the scale. To reach an acceptable level of consistency, it is advised to accept only scales for which Cronbach's α is at least α ≥ 0,7, but not much higher than 0,9. Not accepting very high α-values should minimize the threat of item redundancy in which case the included items basically all ask the same question in a different wording (Streiner/Norman 1989). For each construct a factor analysis with orthogonal varimax rotation was run to support the results from the reliability analysis with Cronbach's α. The factor analysis is usually used to discover patterns in the relationships between items (Darlington et al. 1973).

Control variables. Activity 3 included the 12-item CSE scale to measure the participant's general job satisfaction, job performance, life satisfaction and locus of control (internal/external), and a 5-item scale to measure the participant's level of Altruism. Furthermore, funnel-debriefing questions (Stapel et al. 2002) were included to ask about the participant's awareness of the priming manipulation and purposes of the study. Two participants reported that they were aware of the manipulation and had to be discarded prior to the data analysis. Additionally, participants were asked to provide background information about gender, age, whether English was their native language, work experience, country of origin and the degree and programme they were currently studying. The control variables were included to provide additional explanations for the effects on the dependent variables.

Coding strategy for qualitative data. The qualitative data in the four above-mentioned open-ended items[1] was evaluated by roughly following the steps of an inductive analysis (Patton 2002, Lee 1999). In the first step, data was repeatedly reviewed while more data was collected in further trials of the experiment. This served to assign first-order codes on emerging topics in a way that all obtained qualitative data could be coded into a category by the end of the data collection. If new codes emerged, data was re-coded where necessary. For the second step, a minimum frequency for all coding categories (i.e. the minimal aggregated number of times that codes in the same category were mentioned in the written answers) of 8 was determined as suggested in Anderson (2007). Any category below this threshold was excluded from the further analysis. This procedure allowed condensing the extensive collected data. In a third step, underlying themes for the categories were developed for the further discussion.

---

[1] Multiple answers were possible.

The goal of this analysis was to explore major themes in the participants' argumentation strategies why a decision to take credit for someone else's idea would be right or wrong.

4. Results

4.1 Quantitative results[2]

Developing scales. For each construct, the scale with the highest α was chosen after comparison with the results from the factor analysis. For *Willingness to take credit* (**Scale 1**), three items were included (α = 0.895), asking about the likelihood the subject would think and consider taking credit for the colleague's idea and how frequently he/she would think about it. For *Willingness to take credit with escalating severity of consequences* (**Scale 2**), three items were included (α= 0.926[3]), asking the subject stepwise if he/she would consider it under anticipation that not taking credit would result in not being promoted, a demotion or being fired. For *Perceived ethical costs* (**Scale 3**), four items were selected (α = 0.886), asking if taking credit is the right thing to do, if it is fair and ethical and if one should feel ashamed about it. For *Perception of others' mindset* (**Scale 4**), three items were included (α = 0.812), asking whether another teammate in the same situation would consider taking credit for the colleague's idea, if he/she would do so under anticipation of a demotion or a dismissal (as a consequence of not taking credit) and how frequently this teammate would think about it. The factor analyses showed similar results (in the rotated factor matrix) and supported the scale development based on Cronbach's α

Manipulation check. The item asking participants whether they feel rather competitive or cooperative (on a scale from 1 to 7, "1" being rather competitive, "7" being rather cooperative) was included to check for priming effects. Ideally, participants in the competitive condition should on average yield a lower mean than in the neutral condition and participants in the cooperative condition a higher mean than the control group. However, participants in the competitive condition (M = 4.22 ; SD = 1.31) did not feel significantly more competitive than in the neutral condition (M = 4.39 ; SD = 1.24), t (34) = - 0.392, p = 0.698, d = 0.13. Also, participants in the cooperative condition (M = 4.47 ; SD = 1.39) did not feel significantly more cooperative than they did in the neutral condition (M = 4.39 ; SD = 1.24), t(35) = - 0.195 , p = 0.846 , d = 0.06.

Hypotheses. Independent-samples t-tests were used to test the hypotheses. Unexpectedly, none of the four hypotheses was supported. Participants in the competitive condition (M = 2.43 ; SD = 0.94) were not more *willing to take credit for someone else's idea* than in the neutral condition (M = 2.65 ; SD = 1.38), t (38) = - 0.581, p = 0.564, d = 0.19. Also, participants in the cooperative condition (M = 2.67 ; SD = 1.45) were not less willing than in the

---
[2] Table 1 (Correlations) and Table 2 (Means and Standard Deviations) can be found in the appendix
[3] Items were used for this scale despite the high α, because an item redundancy as consequence of alternating wording is not expected: The items address all negative, but different consequences.

neutral condition, t (40) = - 0.038 , p = 0.970 , d = 0.01 (**Hypothesis 1**)[4]. Participants in the competitive condition (M = 3.27 ; SD = 1.48) were also not more *willing to take credit for someone else's idea with escalating severity of consequences* than the participants in the neutral condition (M = 3.25 ; SD = 1.79), t (38) = 0.032, p = 0.975, d = 0.01. Participants in the cooperative condition (M = 3.39 ; SD = 1.58) were also not less willing under *escalating severity of consequences* than they were in the neutral condition, t (40) = - 0.277 , p = 0.783 , d = 0.08 (**Hypothesis 2**). Similarly, participants in the competitive condition (M = 1.31 ; SD = 0.49) did not *perceive* less *ethical costs* than the participants in the neutral condition (M = 1.39 ; SD = 0.60), t (38) = - 0.433 , p = 0.668 , d = 0.15 . Participants in the cooperative condition (M = 1.42 ; SD = 0.91) did also not *perceive* more *ethical costs* than in the neutral condition, t (40) = - 0.136 , p = 0.892, d = 0.04 (**Hypothesis 3**). Finally, participants in the competitive condition (M = 4.12 ; SD = 1.16) did not *perceive others' mindsets* to be more competitive than in the neutral condition (M = 4.12 ; SD = 1.07), t (38) = .000 , p = 1.000 , d = 0. Likewise, participants in the cooperative condition (M = 4.53 ; SD = 1.10) did not perceive others to have a more cooperative mindset than in the neutral condition, t (40) = - 1.231 , p = 0.226 , d = 0.38 (**Hypothesis 4**).

Control variables and inter-scale correlations. Interestingly, Table 1 shows significant correlations between the four scales and certain control variables. As the priming conditions were found to have no significant effect on the outcome variables, some additional multiple linear regression analyses were conducted to further explore the correlations between the scales. As suggested by Allen and Bennett (2008), the necessary assumptions (multicollinearity, multivariate outliers, normality of residuals, linearity and homoscedasticity) for the regressions with the respective variables were tested. The original independent variables, the priming or neutral conditions, were not considered in these regressions. Control variables were included as predictors if a correlation with the respective scale existed and if deemed to be supported by theory. All predictor variables were entered directly into the regressions.

For Scale 1, a regression with the three other scales and Altruism (one-way ANOVA: F (4 , 57) = 17.6, p = 0.000) showed that the predictors explained 55.3 % of the variance. It yielded significant effects for Scale 2, t (57) = 3.32, β 0.367, p = 0.002, and for Scale 4, t (57) = 4.05 β = 0.422, p = 0.000. So, participants with higher scores on willingness to take credit with

---

[4] The item which asked participants about the percentaged chance with which he or she would take credit for the colleague's idea positively correlated with Scale 1 (β = 0.642, p = 0.000). The item was included to check if the participants' answers for items with the Likert response format deviate from the answer on the same topic on a continuous scale.

escalating severity and on perception of others' mindsets were also more willing to take credit for someone else's idea in the first place. Altruism and Scale 3 were not shown to have a significant effect on Scale 1.

For Scale 2, the predictors Scale 1, Scale 3, Scale 4, Altruism and Origin Anglo-Saxon and Western Europe countries explained 49,7 % of the variance (one-way ANOVA: $F (5, 56) = 11.05$, $p = 0.000$). Scale 1 ($t (56) = 3.36$; $\beta = 0.436$; $p = 0.001$) and marginally also Origin Anglo Saxon and Western European countries ($t (56) = 1.98$; $\beta = 0.330$; $p = 0.053$) had an effect. Therefore, participants who were more willing to take credit for someone else's idea and originated from an Anglo-Saxon or Western European country were also more willing to take credit for this idea if they had to anticipate negative repercussion in case they would not take credit for the idea. The other scales and Altruism did not have a significant effect.

The regression for Scale 3 entailed the three other scales, *Altruism, Origin Anglo- Saxon and Western Europe* and *Origin Asia* as predictors. The two latter variables were included to see if there is a cultural difference regarding taking credit for someone else's ideas and norm violations as suggested by Chin and Spindel (2009). Although the one-way ANOVA was significant for $p \leq 0.05$ ($F (6,55) = 2.36$)), the predictor variables did not show any significant effects on Scale 3.

Finally, Scale 1 and Scale 2 were regressed against Scale 4. The ANOVA ($F (2, 59) = 23.89$; $p = 0.000$) showed that 44.7 % of the variance of Scale 1 could be explained by the predictors. Only Scale 1 yielded a significant effect, $t (59) = 3.997$, $\beta = 0.504$; $p = 0.000$. This showed that participants with a high willingness to take credit for someone else's idea also perceive others to have a similar mindset as they do.

4.2 Qualitative results

In the inductive analysis three major themes underlying the identified coding categories clearly emerged: *individual level, victim and group level* and a *normative level*. In addition, the coding category *same rationale* was also included for further support. The three themes included both answers from the items about the participants' arguments and about the participants' anticipation of the teammate's arguments. The theme *individual level* was chosen for 9 coding categories because they all somehow related to personal costs incurred by the participant (or the random teammate) for taking or not taking credit for the idea. This included negative consequences for taking credit for someone else's idea (e.g. punishment [n = 10, n(T)[5] = 12], a deteriorated personal relationship to the victim [n = 13, n(T) = 9]), or the team [n(T) = 8]), the avoidance of negative job outcomes (n= 15, n(T) = 20) and a negative social exchange relationship with the victim (n = 8). 16 participants also expected a random teammate to take credit because advancing in his/her career would simply come first. Remarkably, the participants' arguments greatly resembled the arguments they would expect from another random teammate in the same situation.

The *victim and group* level included three categories that were not directly unrelated to the individual taking credit for the idea. They focused on the argumentation that taking credit for someone else's idea would clearly present a violation of group norms. That would deteriorate the climate for all team members (n = 10). Another major argument in this category was that it would mainly harm the victim (n = 9). The only viable reason for taking credit would be that the victim deserved it due to a prior wrongdoing (n(T) = 10) irrespective of whom was harmed.

The *normative level* contained three categories that referred to universal statements regardless which person or group would be specifically harmed by the action. It was argued that such an action would be always wrong (n = 11) and universally unethical (n = 17). The random teammate was also expected to consider it in general as unethical (n(T) = 30).

The coding category *same rationale* could be applied 8 times, encompassing all answers that stated that a random teammate would follow the same reasoning as the participant.

Table 3 provides an overview over the coding categories and themes.

---

[5] (T) indicates a coding category referring to the expected argumentation of a random teammate in the same situation

Table 3: Coding categories and themes with definitions and frequencies

Code	Definition	Frequency
Coding categories for "personal level"		
Benefit in critical situations	It would be **right** if it was necessary for the participant's own personal benefit in critical situations (promotion, performance appraisal etc.).	15
Negative exchange relationship	It would be **right** if the victim has previously violated the personal relationship with the participant.	8
Relationship with victim threatened	It would be **not right** because the participant expects negative consequences for the future relationship with the victim	13
Anticipation of negative consequences	It would be **not right** because the participant anticipates negative consequences if his/her action is discovered (e.g. punishment, retaliation).	10
(T) Avoidance of negative job outcomes*	The teammate would think: It is a **necessary evil** to avoid negative job outcomes (demotion, dismissal etc.).	20
(T) Advancement in one's career	The teammate would think: It **is right**, because advancing in his/her career comes first.	16
(T) Anticipation of negative consequences	The teammate would think: It **is not right**, because there could negative consequences if my action is discovered.	12
(T) Relationship with victim threatened	The teammate would think: It **is not right**, because this would hurt my relationship with the victim.	9
(T) Relationship with rest of team	The teammate would think: It **is not right**, because this would hurt my relationship with the whole team.	8
Coding categories for "victim & group level"		
Victim deserves it in general	It would **be right** if the victim deserves it in general due to something in the past (not necessarily related to the personal relationship with the participant).	10
Violation of group norms & deterioration of group climate	It is **not right** because taking credit for the victim's idea is a violation of group norms and results in a deterioration of the overall climate in the team.	13
(T) Harm to victim	The teammate would think: It is **not right**, because it is harmful to the victim.	9
Coding categories for "normative level"		
Always wrong	It would be **never right** to take credit for someone else's idea.	11
Universally unethical	It is **not right**, because it is generally unethical.	17
(T) Unethically	The teammate would think: It is **not right**, because taking credit for someone else's idea is unethical.	30
Coding category for "same perception"		
Same rationale	The teammate is expected to follow the same reasoning as the participant.	8

*Coding categories marked with a (T) contain answers to the items referring to the expected argumentation of a random teammate in the same situation

5. Discussion

Rejected hypotheses. No support could be found for any of the four hypotheses. Remarkably, although there was no significant effect, the means of the priming conditions point into an unexpected, opposite direction: on average, participants in the cooperative condition were more willing to take credit for the colleague's idea than participants in the other conditions. They also perceived on average less ethical costs (a higher mean indicates less ethical costs perceived) and expected other people's mindset as more competitive than the participants in the other conditions did. Despite these unexpected results, there are several reasons, which might explain the failure of the priming procedure.

Control variables. The priming effects could have been overwritten by the participants' personal disposition. Altruism und CSE were included in the first place to control for the assumption that there might be an effect from the participant's personality. Altruism as part of the Big 5 dimension *Agreeableness* is expected to account for a more pro-social, cooperative behaviour (Penner et al. 1995). Participants with a high level of Altruism are therefore expected to be less willing to take credit for someone else's idea regardless the prime influence. CSE was included due to a study by Brunborg (2008), which had two relevant findings: First, it confirmed that job demands are positively related to stress. Second, it showed that persons with a high CSE score tend to perceive less job stress. The above mentioned *general strain* theory by Agnew assumes that stress urges individuals to look for alternative ways to reduce the source of stress (the overwhelming job demands). Therefore, participants in the present study with higher CSE scores were expected to be less willing to take credit for another person's idea. They would not tend to associate exceeding job demands with higher levels of stress in the first place. As shown in Table 1, CSE positively correlated with the variables Age, Tenure and Origin Anglo-Saxon and Western Europe. Following the thought that more mature and experienced individuals possess higher CSE scores, those individuals could also have a disposition that *protects* them against the influence from subtle social cues. However, none of these control variables did have any effect on the dependent variables (CSE, Age and Tenure were included in initial regressions, but removed afterwards due to their weak and insignificant effect). Solely, originating from an Anglo-Saxon or Western European country explained some of the variance of Scale 2, whereby this effect was only marginally significant due to a p-value being slightly higher than the critical value. The effect could be still coincidental.

Other possible explanations. It is more likely that personal dispositions were responsible for the refutation of the hypotheses that were not captured by this study's control variables. Hertel and Fiedler (1998) e.g. not only tested the influence from primes, but also the consistency of social value orientations of their subjects in a sequence of allocation tasks. They were able to show that only participants with an unstable social value orientation were successfully influenced by primes (Hertel/Fielder 1998). Building on that, Smeesters et al. (2003) found that priming only produced more cooperation for those participants that did not show a strong pro-self orientation. This is especially relevant for an explanation for the refutation of Hypothesis 3: An individual orientation towards a certain value could have influenced which values are considered important in the ethical decision-making process. Although the experimenter in preparation of this study was aware of these findings, measuring the social value orientations would have exceeded the experiment's available resources.

Another factor that was not captured was the participants' level of stress while they took part in the experiment. It can be assumed that the participants were not stressed by the conditions of the experiment. However, each participant was in a very intense and stressful preparation for the final exams of their Master degrees or – in the case of the PhD students –in a similar situation. In fact, a study by Storbeck and Clore (2008) found that a negative mood or affect inhibits semantic and affective priming. Assuming that those participants were more or less negatively affected by the exam period, the overall stress level could have minimized the impact of the priming effect.

Flawed priming procedure. Another reason could have been the experimental set-up of the priming procedure. In contrast to the other studies that were considered for the present study, the items for the independent variables were far more numerous: although the original priming tasks, that have been shown to be effective in other studies, were used, their influence might just have been too weak to suffice for the entire questionnaire. In Kay et al. (2004) participants were e.g. only asked four questions about a hypothetical scenario after the priming procedures. Still, if that was the case, there should have been at least an effect on the first items, which were used for Scale 1.
The hypothetical scenario might also have been to unambiguous. As initially mentioned, priming procedures work best in highly ambiguous situations. Despite the efforts of the experimenter to keep the scenario as ambiguous as possible (very limited information about the working conditions in the firm and about the involved persons and a unisex name for the

colleague), the obvious action of taking credit for someone else's idea might have been enough to bias the participants.

The order of the items also could have had a negative effect on the priming procedure. Kay and Ross (2003: 634) found that the "prime-to-behaviour link" could be enhanced if the participants were asked to actively construe the hypothetical situation in question right after being subliminally primed. In particular, they were asked to rate the appropriateness of names for a subsequent prisoner dilemma game. They found that e.g. the participants in the competitive condition who chose a competitive name for the game also revealed more competitive intentions in the game afterwards than without the intermediate construal. Likewise, the manipulation check, which asked participants about their feelings in the present study, could have had a similar effect if positioned before the scenario. The participants would have had to actively construe their feelings. Thus, the priming effect might have been significant in the present study.

Inter-scale effects. However, the data showed other, unintended findings that can partially explain the study's outcomes. The multiple effects from the four scales on each other are consistent with some initial theoretical considerations. The mutual effects of Scale 1 and Scale 2 on each other acknowledged that if there is a basic willingness to choose taking credit for someone else's idea as an alternative to cope with job demands, it is also likely to increase if the consequences for not doing it get worse. Furthermore, Scale 1 is obviously a predictor (with the highest standardized beta coefficient in this study) of Scale 4. Therefore, the theoretical assumption that people expect other people to have similar attitudes or ways of thinking was supported. As Scale 4 also had a positive effect on Scale 1, it can be also expected that the mere anticipation that others are also likely to take credit for the idea increases one's own willingness to do that. In addition, the relatively large R^2 (0.553, 0.497, 0.447) in the regressions indicate that the Scales present viable explanatory variables for the outcomes.

Except the unsatisfying findings for perceived ethical costs, the above-mentioned inter-scale correlations suggest that the study successfully addressed themes that are relevant to the study's topic: stealing ideas from each other to cope with job demands. The question remains which factor is able to predict the kind of individual who is more likely to be willing to take credit for someone else's idea or who expects someone else to think like that.

Qualitative results. The purpose of the open-ended items was to explore the underlying reasoning in the participant's decision-making process, i.e. to understand how they justify (in which cases) taking credit for the colleague's idea is right or not right. First, a major finding in these results is the congruence of the participant's arguments on the *personal level* with the expected arguments of another random teammate in the same situation. In addition, eight participants mentioned that they would expect others to follow the same rationale. This further supports the findings about the relationships between Scale 1 and Scale 4.

Second, not only universally ethical (on a *normative level*) and altruistic concerns ("It is not right, because it is harmful to the victim"), but also many arguments, which were related to personal negative consequences that might follow, appeared. Thus, it can be assumed that the question if taking credit for someone else's idea is right or not right is not restricted to ethics, but also entails a person's utility considerations: even a person that does not identify this action as an ethical issue might still consider it wrong because it negatively affects the person's relationship to others or his or her career perspectives. This missing differentiation could have been responsible for the insignificant results for *Perceived ethical costs*.

Third, the theme of retaliation and revenge emerged. Several participants considered the action as right if the victim had a negative social exchange relationship with either the participant or another person on the team. This argument implicates a "denial of victim" (Anand et al. 2005: 10), i.e. the colleague of whom the idea is copied from did something bad in the past and therefore deserves it. Interestingly, this negative social exchange relationship has not necessarily to exist between the person who retaliates and the person who is responsible for the e.g. prior unfair treatment. The retaliating person could also have been merely an observer (without being the victim) of the unfair treatment and now wishes to teach the offender a lesson (Skarlicki/Folger 2004).

The goal of the qualitative part of this paper was not to develop theory, but to help to refine further research on the present topic. In fact, these findings deliver valuable implications for future research, which will be discussed in the conclusion of this paper.

6. Limitations

There are three main limitations for the quantitative part in this study that have to be considered. The sample group presents the first limitation. In contrast to the studies from which the priming tasks were taken from, the sample included multiple native languages. Only about one third (n = 21, p = 33.9 %) spoke English as a native language. Although there was no effect found, this could have impeded the semantic priming effect. Even if non-native English speakers knew a particular priming word, they might not associate it with the same concept a native English speaker would do. Additionally, the size of the sample group was very small with about only 20 participants per independent variable. Looking at the very small effect sizes in independent-samples t-tests used to test the hypotheses, more participants would have been required to re-establish the necessary statistical power (Aron/Aron 1999). Also, due to the small sample size it was not really feasible to explore the impact of cultural differences with participants coming from 24 different countries. Furthermore, the sample was taken from only one institution and only from students in post-graduate studies. However, the sample group is representative insofar as the students are likely to go into knowledge worker jobs after their studies.

The second limitation is the hypothetical moral situation the participants are confronted with. As Straughan (1975) stresses a major issue with this kind of scenarios is that they lack immediacy: In contrast to real life, a hypothetical situation does not allow to incorporate the personal motivation of an individual to choose a decision over another. The personal motivation is rather determined by his or her situational reasoning, motives and the individual's psychological state. Furthermore, the inevitable kind of questions that are related to those situations allow different interpretations: A "what would you do…" question could either mean "What do you predict your action would be…?" (Prediction) or "What decision do you think you ought to make?" (Actual decision) (Straughan 1975: 185). This could have caused different interpretations of the questions and therefore, affected the participants' responses. Also, the moral judgment about a hypothetical third person (like the other random teammate in the same situation) is not likely to deliver realistic results without providing detailed information about this person. Even with that information, Straughan points that "situational feelings of this kind cannot be experienced secondhand" (Straughan 1975: 188). This might be also a possible explanation why the participants expected others to have a similar mindset in this scenario.

The last limitation was already mentioned in the previous chapter. Several aspects of the participants' personal disposition that could have accounted for the results have not been measured like the individual social value orientations and their consistency, which was shown in previous studies to affect the priming effects (Hertel/Fiedler 1998 ; Smeesters et al. 2003 ; Utz et al. 2004). Also, the stage of moral development (Kohlberg/Lickona 1976) of each participant was not measured. As the moral development is not necessarily related to age, this could have given further insights into the participants' moral reasoning and another possible explanation for the insignificant results for Hypothesis 3.

The qualitative part holds two limitations. First, the coding process was performed by only one coder (the author of this paper). Therefore, the results might be biased by subjective interpretation. Second, the participants only answered questions about whether the action was right or not right. More insights could have been gained if the participants had had the possibility to explain their decision-making process also in more ways. In fact, some participants mentioned this to the experimenter after they had finished the experiment.

7. Conclusion and implications

The first goal of this study was not met. It could not show that situational influences like primes activate competitive or cooperative processing mindsets that alter an individual's decision to take credit for a colleague's idea. However, despite the various limitations and unexpected findings, this study is still valuable for future research.

First, it was shown that the three scales W*illingness to take credit for someone else's idea*, the *Willingness to take credit for someone else's idea with escalating severity of consequences* and the *Perception of others' mindsets* are suited for further exploring the theme of taking credit for someone else's idea. Future research should therefore focus on the factors that could affect one of those scales in the first place. Next to situational influences, personality traits and personal dispositions beyond altruism and the CSE should be incorporated and measured in its consistency over a series of decisions. This has already been done for social value orientations and delivered significant results. Relevant personality traits might be those, which have been shown to trigger deviant or illegal behaviour, such as narcissism, trait hostility, (low) self-control or (low) conscientiousness (Griffin/O'Leary-Kelly 2004).

Second, the qualitative results help to improve the exploration of the decision-making process, which is involved with taking credit for someone else's idea. As mentioned, it is uncertain if individuals even perceive this action as a moral issue. The person of whom the idea is taken from might not be even considered as a victim. To overcome this uncertainty, future research should refine the examination of the decision-making process by clearly distinguishing between ethical motives and an utilitarian cost-benefit analysis of possible implications of a decision. Additionally, the social exchange relationship between the involved persons should be clearly stated in advance to avoid any undesired assumptions by the participants. Furthermore, while looking at ethical motives, the results also suggest to distinguish between altruistic concerns ("It is not right, because it is harmful to the victim") and universal ethical concerns ("It would be never right to take credit for someone else's idea."). All in all, a more sophisticated approach could be able to explain why no significant results for the perceived ethical costs were found in this study.

Future research should also pay closer attention to the sensitive priming procedure. Next to the avoidance of flaws mentioned in the discussion of the results, the inclusion of the valence of the words might lead to better results. Hertel and Fiedler (1998) found that there is in fact a difference whether words are positively or negatively associated with cooperation or competition. Prime words with a negative valence for cooperation are e.g. *dependent*, *exploited* or *adjusted*. Words with a positive valence can be *constructive*, *helpful* or *tolerant* (Hertel/Fiedler 1998: 56).

Finally, if a hypothetical scenario is used, it should be made as unambiguous as possible to ensure the effectiveness of the primes. The question is if a hypothetical scenario followed by a questionnaire can produce the required level of unambiguousness. Future research might therefore consider alternative methods like interactive role-plays or group exercises subsequent to individually priming the participants. This way, participants might be less aware that they are dealing with taking credit for someone else's idea. In addition, the participants would be both more physically and mentally involved in the situation by interacting with other people. Thus, the weaknesses of a hypothetical scenario can be minimized and produce significant and results closer to reality.

Appendix

Material used in the experiment

Activity 1

Competitive priming condition

Task 1: Word Search Puzzle

In this task you have a puzzle with 12 hidden words. A list of the hidden words is provided below. Please try to find as many of the hidden words and mark them within the puzzle.

Please mind that words can go diagonal, horizontal and vertical and both backward and forward. They may also cross each other.

```
Y G C D R M O E P T F Y S A B
R C H A I R K P O V O P I K W
L R N N R A C U E T E P M O C
A A I Q P G R F I V E Y U A R
V D W Y T N T Y G Y I C W N L
I I U M A S Q N Z S V S Q J C
R O D M S Q E R O B J J J B D
C I E T I H V T X O E A S G O
V N A A D O C N N L Z P X U J
T M A B F V Q L T O V U M S R
P S R W I M P T R N C H C R K
L M X N R A A U Q M M A F X B
E P M L A B G J L K H X H N C
H W Z P L O N I J V X Z L U T
K O O B G F C F T H E F J R K
```

BATTLE
BOOK
CHAIR
COMPETE
CONTEST
DIARY
LAMP
RADIO
RIVALRY
STAMP
TOURNAMENT
WIN

Task 2: Scrambled Sentences

In this task you have 24 sentences. Each of the sentences contains 5 randomly placed words. The purpose of this assignment is to form a correct sentence or phrase **with only four of the five words.**

For example: You have the following words: *brown, the, memory, is, closet*. From those words you can create a whole sentence: '*The closet is brown*'.
OR you have the following words: *observe, a, from, nice, painting*. You could create the following phrase: '*observe a nice painting*'.
Please write down your sentences or phrases on the dotted lines.

1. it, bears, sometimes, aggressive, are

....

2. disliked, enemy, his, he, is

....

3. brown, play, desk, the, is

....

4. you, gave, rank, three, number

....

5. everyone, him, Bob, else, outwitted

....

6. long, the, today, is, book

....

7. is, the, office, lawyer, rich

....

8. ball, the, hoop, toss, normally

....

9. very, be, can, manipulative, cats

....

10. theory, a, paper, Darwin, had

....

11. helpless, it, hides, there, over

....

12. competition, he, well, the, won

....

13. weather, needs, power, more, California

....

14. sky, the, seamless, is, red

....

15. wrestler, the ,fierce, in, looked

....

16. today, is, tournament, often, the

....

17. animals, with, are, inconsiderate, skunks

....

18. send, I, mail, it, over

....

19. lose, money, wallet, your, never

....

20. ongoing, it, battle, the, is

....

21. lions, field, scary, are, vicious

....

22. Pat, today, capitalist, very, is

....

23. big, chairs, they, box, are

....

24. boss, office, my, cut-throat, is

....

Cooperative priming condition

Task 1: Word Search Puzzle

In this task you have a puzzle with 12 hidden words. A list of the hidden words is provided below. Please try to find as many of the hidden words and mark them within the puzzle.

Please mind that words can go diagonal, horizontal and vertical and both backward and forward. They may also cross each other.

```
P P V Y E C C G B B E C T G S
P O M W L H W Y O L A O O R T
L J X A A P G Q O K P M G O A
T Y K I L Y A M K W S M E U M
N P R M Y L Q P Z F V U T P P
U O A K U N W L C R Y N H K X
V E N W T S M F E R I E E L E
T B Q D V I Q X A J E P R Q O
R D Z U P X S I Y J C S O D R
U D Z T W A D Y K X J H V Y O
O A R X B E J M T B B A X K U
R A D I O E P E B Y X R U A V
D Q W K K F I M A Y Q I K V X
R Q I H J N D Q F N W N R J H
C O O P E R A T I O N G D I O
```

BOOK
CHAIR
COMMUNE
COOPERATION
DIARY
GROUP
LAMP
RADIO
SHARING
STAMP
TEAM
TOGETHER

Task 2: Scrambled Sentences

In this task you have 24 sentences. Each of the sentences contains 5 randomly placed words. The purpose of this assignment is to form a correct sentence or phrase **with only four of the five words.**

For example: You have the following words: *brown, the, memory, is, closet*. From those words you can create a whole sentence: '*The closet is brown*'.
OR you have the following words: *observe, a, from, nice, painting*. You could create the following phrase: '*observe a nice painting*'.
Please write down your sentences or phrases on the dotted lines.

1. helped, friend, computer, she, her

....

2. sky, the, seamless, red, is

....

3. harmony, perfect, have, often, they

....

4. the, machine, washes, frequently, clothes

....

5. created, was, start, alliance, the

....

6. misses, Jared, family, his, sunlight

....

7. send, mailed, I, over, it

....

8. looks, house, the, fair, nice

....

9. pact, boys, they, a, had

....

10. ball, the, hoop, toss, normally

....

11. medicine, warm, doctors, demeanours, have

....

12. though, needs, policeman, cooperation, the

....

13. somewhat, prepared, I, was, retired

....

14. light, distribute, turn, the, off

....

15. farming, formed, community, they, a

....

16. easily, paper, store, ripped, the

....

17. ruling, reasonable, the, was, still

....

18. she, agree, to, book, had

....

19. apartment, they, the, window, cleaned

....

20. the, was, mutual, if, decision

....

21. enough, they, just, had, was

....

22. carefully, the, listened, or, student

....

23. joined, he, tomorrow, brotherhood, the

....

24. learn, children, share, June, to

....

Neutral condition

Task 1: Word Search Puzzle

In this task you have a puzzle with 12 hidden words. A list of the hidden words is provided below. Please try to find as many of the hidden words and mark them within the puzzle.

Please mind that words can go diagonal, horizontal and vertical and both backward and forward. They may also cross each other.

P D I A M O N D F Z U L O V E
I Q H D X M J L O B I I P I R
N W G R W I N D O W D S P L U
D I A R Y B U B L A K K D B T
N F P G N T S A R C M O L N C
S R C Z K P J G J M V V O D I
C C N Q P H K T O X N N Z B P
S H S A O A P U E G N R V G M
T V A J Z T Q T U Q F B N F E
A P C I T P X T J U L W U X M
M A S A R P M A L U E X C M Y
P M I O R W O P E E W A Y K R
I B D M M P I J Y X V W Q O V
Y I Q I Q Z E Y B V N C N B I
P M D Q J L K T G K V Z S T U

BLUE
BOOK
CARPET
CHAIR
DIAMOND
DIARY
HAT
LAMP
PICTURE
RADIO
STAMP
WINDOW

Task 2: Scrambled Sentences

In this task you have 24 sentences. Each of the sentences contains 5 randomly placed words. The purpose of this assignment is to form a correct sentence or phrase **with only four of the five words.**

For example: You have the following words: *brown, the, memory, is, closet*. From those words you can create a whole sentence: '*The closet is brown*'.

OR you have the following words: *observe, a, from, nice, painting*. You could create the following phrase: '*observe a nice painting*'.

Please write down your sentences or phrases on the dotted lines.

1. person, one, big, angular, is

   ....

2. glasses, the, can, through, watch

   ....

3. a, relationship, in, long, banal

   ....

4. his, saw, animal, she, often

   ....

5. role, a, in, late, small

   ....

6. boy, fat, the, is, skew

   ....

7. mail, long, sending, flag, a

   ....

8. ostrich, has, is, enormous, the

   ....

9. cold, round, stiff, the, from

   ....

10. drop, the, pen, kiss, you

    ....

11. a, as, on, normal, manner

....

12. making, healthy, a, bike, walk

....

13. slow, was, she, very, close

....

14. shut, your, are, mouth, ears

....

15. window, the, full, is, colourless

....

16. flat, tired, quite, you, feel

....

17. slim, very, a, tall, person

....

18. everything, a, sides, time, has

....

19. eggs, a, are, oval, these

....

20. black, in, head, light, the

....

21. the, reed, agile, cyclist, fell

....

22. you, iron, wash, clothes, your

....

23. edge, thin, wall, the, is

....

24. opposite, are, smart, others, because

....

Activity 2

Please carefully read the following scenario prior to answering the questions that follow.

> On Monday, your boss asks you and your teammates to each develop an advertising campaign idea for a new product that your firm is about to release to the market. Your boss has asked everybody to bring their ideas to the team meeting on Friday afternoon.
>
> On Wednesday, you accidentally overhear Sam, one of your teammates, talking on the phone to a colleague from another department about the advertising campaign for the new product. Sam does not know that you are overhearing the phone conversation. While speaking to the colleague on the phone, Sam communicates, in great detail, the advertising campaign idea that Sam has developed for the new product release. After thinking about Sam's idea, you consider Sam's idea to be quite clever and promising and think that the idea is a great way to promote the new product.
>
> It's Friday, and you know that all of your teammates have at least one good idea of their own to present during the team meeting. Due to your unusually huge workload this week, you have not been able to produce an idea that pleases you, especially one that is as brilliant and exciting as Sam's idea. This is frustrating to you because you typically have good ideas to present. You know that your boss expects every team member to have a good idea to present during the team meeting. From watching your teammates' behaviours in past team meetings, you have observed that Sam presents ideas to the team after all teammates have finished presenting their ideas. This knowledge can give you the opportunity to present before Sam does in the team meeting.

Please turn to the next page and follow the directions provided. The following questions refer to the scenario you just read. Please read the following directions carefully, and answer each question.

Thank you.

To answer question 1 to 3, please indicate your answer for each question by ticking the appropriate box.

Imagine that you know with certainty that you will be the first team member to present in the team meeting on Friday afternoon.

		Not at all likely	Hardly likely	A little likely	Somewhat likely	Moderately likely	Very likely	Extremely likely
1	What is the likelihood that you would think about presenting Sam's good idea to the team as if it is your own idea?	☐	☐	☐	☐	☐	☐	☐
2	What is the likelihood that you would consider taking credit for Sam's idea?	☐	☐	☐	☐	☐	☐	☐
3	What is the likelihood that you would have doubts about taking credit for Sam's idea?	☐	☐	☐	☐	☐	☐	☐
4	What is the likelihood that you would not hesitate to take credit for Sam's idea?	☐	☐	☐	☐	☐	☐	☐
		Never	Very Rarely	Rarely	Occasionally	Frequently	Very Frequently	Always
5	Prior to the team meeting on Friday afternoon, how often during your workday do you think you would consider taking credit for Sam's idea?	☐	☐	☐	☐	☐	☐	☐

For question 6, please estimate the probability from 0 to 100 by filling in the blank in the right column.

6	What do you think the chances are that you would present Sam's idea to the team as if it is your own idea?	I think that there would be a _____ % chance that I would present Sam's idea to the team as if it is my own idea.

For the following questions, please indicate your level of agreement. For each question, tick the appropriate box.

	To what extent do you agree that taking credit for Sam's idea….	Strongly disagree	Disagree	Disagree somewhat	Neutral	Agree somewhat	Agree	Strongly Agree
7	….. is the right thing for you to do?	☐	☐	☐	☐	☐	☐	☐
8	….. is fair?	☐	☐	☐	☐	☐	☐	☐
9	….. is ethical?	☐	☐	☐	☐	☐	☐	☐

To what extent do you agree or disagree to the following arguments?

	Suppose someone argued that taking Sam's idea is the right thing for you to do ……	Strongly disagree	Disagree	Disagree somewhat	Neutral	Agree somewhat	Agree	Strongly Agree
10	…. because there is not much harm done to the team as a whole and therefore it is forgivable.	☐	☐	☐	☐	☐	☐	☐
11	…. because there is nothing to feel ashamed about.	☐	☐	☐	☐	☐	☐	☐
12	…. because considering your huge workload it is a smart thing for you to do.	☐	☐	☐	☐	☐	☐	☐
13	…. because there is nothing to feel guilty about.	☐	☐	☐	☐	☐	☐	☐

Please answer questions 14 and 15 by writing down your answer.

14 Can you think of any other arguments why it would be right to take credit for Sam's idea? <u>Please write your thoughts in the space below.</u>

_____
_____
_____
_____

15 Can you think of any other arguments why it would <u>NOT</u> be right to take credit for Sam's idea? <u>Please write your thoughts in the space below.</u>

_____
_____
_____
_____

To answer question 16 to 19, please indicate your answer for each question by ticking the appropriate box.

	What is the likelihood that you would consider taking credit for Sam's idea if you know that <u>NOT</u> presenting a good idea will result in…..	Not at all likely	Hardly likely	A little likely	Somewhat likely	Moderately likely	Very likely	Extremely likely
16	….. you will receive a poor performance appraisal from your boss.	☐	☐	☐	☐	☐	☐	☐
		Not a all likely	Hardly likely	A little likely	Somewhat likely	Moderately likely	Very likely	Extremely likely

		Not at all likely	Hardly likely	A little likely	Somewhat likely	Moderately likely	Very likely	Extremely likely
17	….. you will not be promoted by your boss as you desire.	☐	☐	☐	☐	☐	☐	☐
18	….. you will be demoted to a lower position by your boss.	☐	☐	☐	☐	☐	☐	☐
19	….. you will be fired by your boss.	☐	☐	☐	☐	☐	☐	☐

Now, please consider that not you, **BUT ANOTHER TEAMMATE** overheard Sam's phone conversation.

Imagine this teammate is the first to present in Friday's team meeting.

		Not at all likely	Hardly likely	A little likely	Somewhat likely	Moderately likely	Very likely	Extremely likely
20	What is the likelihood that your teammate would consider taking credit for Sam's good idea as if it is his/her own idea?	☐	☐	☐	☐	☐	☐	☐
21	What is the likelihood that your teammate would not hesitate to take credit for Sam's idea?	☐	☐	☐	☐	☐	☐	☐
22	What is the likelihood that your teammate would think that taking credit for Sam's idea is the right thing to do?	☐	☐	☐	☐	☐	☐	☐
23	Imagine your teammate is facing a demotion or even a dismissal if he/she does not present a good idea during the team meeting. What is the likelihood that your teammate would consider taking credit for Sam's idea?	☐	☐	☐	☐	☐	☐	☐

		Never	Very Rarely	Rarely	Occasionally	Frequently	Very Frequently	Always
24	Prior to the team meeting on Friday afternoon, how often during his/her workday do you think your teammate would consider taking credit for Sam's idea?	☐	☐	☐	☐	☐	☐	☐

Please answer question 25 and 26 by writing down your answer in the space provided.

25 Why do you believe that your teammate would think that taking credit for Sam's idea is the right thing to do? Please write your thoughts in the space below.

_____
_____
_____
_____

26 Why do you believe that your teammate would think that taking credit for Sam's idea is NOT the right thing to do? Please write your thoughts in the space below.

_____
_____
_____
_____

NOW, PLEASE PUT "ACTIVITY TWO" BACK INTO THE ENVELOPE AND TAKE OUT "ACTIVITY THREE". YOU MAY START TO WORK ON "ACTIVITY THREE" RIGHT AWAY.

Activity 3

To answer the following question, please circle the appropriate number.

On a scale from 1 to 7, "1" being rather competitive and "7" being rather cooperative, how do you feel at this moment?

| rather competitive | 1 | 2 | 3 | 4 | 5 | 6 | 7 | rather cooperative |

Indicate your level of agreement or disagreement with the following statements by ticking the appropriate box.

		Strongly disagree	Disagree	Neutral	Agree	Strongly Agree
1	I am confident I get the success I deserve in life.	☐	☐	☐	☐	☐
2	Sometimes I feel depressed.	☐	☐	☐	☐	☐
3	When I try, I generally succeed.	☐	☐	☐	☐	☐
4	Sometimes when I fail I feel worthless.	☐	☐	☐	☐	☐
5	I complete tasks successfully.	☐	☐	☐	☐	☐
6	Sometimes, I do not feel in control of my work.	☐	☐	☐	☐	☐
7	Overall, I am satisfied with myself.	☐	☐	☐	☐	☐
8	I am filled with doubts about my competence.	☐	☐	☐	☐	☐
9	I determine what will happen in my life.	☐	☐	☐	☐	☐
10	I do not feel in control of my success in my career.	☐	☐	☐	☐	☐
11	I am capable of coping with most of my problems.	☐	☐	☐	☐	☐
12	There are times when things look pretty bleak and hopeless to me.	☐	☐	☐	☐	☐

For the items below please tick the box which best describes your past behaviour.

		Never	Once	More than once	Often	Very Often
13	I have helped carry a stranger's belongings (e.g. bags, books etc.).	☐	☐	☐	☐	☐
14	I have allowed someone to go ahead of me in a queue.	☐	☐	☐	☐	☐
15	I have let a neighbour whom I didn't know too well borrow an item of some value (e.g. tools, dishes)	☐	☐	☐	☐	☐
16	I have, before being asked, voluntarily looked after a neighbour's pets or children without being paid for it.	☐	☐	☐	☐	☐

DEBRIEFING & BACKGROUND INFORMATION

1. What do you think is the purpose of this study? <u>Please write down your answer in the space below.</u>

_____
_____
_____
_____

Please indicate the correct response that best represents you for the following questions by ticking the appropriate box. For questions 4, 9 and 10 please write down your answer in the spaces provided below.

2. Do you think that any of the tasks you performed have been related to each other?

    Yes ☐   No ☐

3. Do you think your performance on one task may have affected your performance on the next task?

    Yes ☐   No ☐

4. Did anything about the study seem strange or suspicious to you?

    Yes ☐   No ☐

    If yes, please specify:

    _____
    _____
    _____

5. Gender: ☐ Female   ☐ Male

6. Age_____ (Please enter your age in years.)

7. Is English your first language? Yes ☐   No ☐

8. How many months and years of work experience do you have? (So, for example if you have worked for 1 year and six months put 1 and 6)

    ___ (years) ___ (months)

9. What is your country of origin?
    _____

10. Which degree and progamme are you currently studying? (e.g. MSc Economics)
    _____

Table 1: Correlations

		Competitive condition	Neutral condition	Cooperative condition	Scale 1	Scale 2	Scale 3	Scale 4	CSE
Neutral condition	r	-.476**	1						
	Sig. (2-tailed)	.000							
Cooperative condition	r	-.512**	-.512**	1					
	Sig. (2-tailed)	.000	.000						
Scale 1	r	-.084	.035	.048	1				
	Sig. (2-tailed)	.517	.786	.713					
Scale 2	r	-.017	-.025	.041	.642**	1			
	Sig. (2-tailed)	.893	.849	.751	.000				
Scale 3	r	-.063	.013	.049	.257	.250	1		
	Sig. (2-tailed)	.627	.923	.704	.044	.050			
Scale 4	r	-.092	-.092	.180	.647**	.546**	.140	1	
	Sig. (2-tailed)	.477	.477	.162	.000	.000	.278		
CSE	r	-.246	.154	.090	-.108	.095	-.068	.084	1
	Sig. (2-tailed)	.054	.231	.488	.403	.462	.598	.515	
Altruism	r	-.016	-.124	.137	-.213	-.240	-.255	-.057	.112
	Sig. (2-tailed)	.901	.338	.289	.096	.061	.045	.662	.385
MSc IER&HRM / HRM	r	-.005	.066	-.060	.009	.069	-.126	.092	.293*
	Sig. (2-tailed)	.972	.611	.644	.944	.592	.329	.477	.021
Any MSc in Politics, Development Studies or else	r	.066	-.013	-.052	-.207	-.176	-.175	-.320*	-.170
	Sig. (2-tailed)	.610	.922	.687	.107	.170	.174	.011	.185
Any PhD programme	r	-.156	-.156	.304*	.054	-.028	-.014	-.008	.041
	Sig. (2-tailed)	.227	.227	.016	.675	.830	.916	.948	.753
Any MSc in Economics	r	-.060	.146	-.084	.191	.027	.123	.170	-.165
	Sig. (2-tailed)	.645	.257	.515	.137	.836	.341	.186	.201

44

		Altruism	MSc: IER&HRM / HRM	Any MSc in Politics, Development Studies or else	Any PhD programme	Any MSc in Economics	Origin: Anglo-Saxon and Western Europe	Origin: Asia
Origin: Anglo-Saxon and Western Europe	r	-.020	-.020	.039	.082	.232	-.232	.171	.254
	Sig. (2-tailed)	.876	.876	.761	.527	.070	.070	.184	.046
Origin: Asia	r	.205	-.125	-.078	.035	.017	.267	.023	-.250
	Sig. (2-tailed)	.110	.333	.547	.789	.894	.036	.862	.050
Origin: Russia and CEE	r	-.109	.008	.099	-.051	-.132	-.020	-.029	-.201
	Sig. (2-tailed)	.398	.954	.443	.692	.305	.878	.824	.118
Gender (female)	r	.163	.163	-.318	.026	-.084	.053	-.011	-.171
	Sig. (2-tailed)	.206	.206	.012	.843	.516	.682	.935	.183
Age	r	.041	-.228	.183	-.060	-.060	-.016	.048	.273
	Sig. (2-tailed)	.753	.075	.155	.645	.644	.902	.712	.032
English native speaker	r	.016	-.129	.110	-.117	-.139	-.193	-.089	-.071
	Sig. (2-tailed)	.899	.316	.393	.366	.282	.133	.493	.585
Tenure (months)	r	.105	-.221	.113	-.201	-.108	-.122	.038	.284
	Sig. (2-tailed)	.415	.084	.380	.116	.404	.346	.768	.025
MSc: IER&HRM / HRM	r	.123	1						
	Sig. (2-tailed)	.340	0						
Any MSc in Politics, Development Studies or else	r	-.147**	-.485**	1					
	Sig. (2-tailed)	.255	.000	0					
Any PhD programme	r	.107	-.185	-.133	1				
	Sig. (2-tailed)	.409	.149	.303	0				
Any MSc in Economics	r	-.079	-.316	-.227	-.087	1			
	Sig. (2-tailed)	.541	.012	.076	.502	0			
Origin: Anglo-Saxon and	r	.058	-.140	-.002	.198	-.050	1		

		Origin: Asia	Origin: Russia and CEE	Gender (female)	Age	English native speaker	Tenure (months)
Origin: Asia	r	1	-.615**	.028	-.054	-.122	.022
	Sig. (2-tailed)		.000	.830	.677	.346	.864
Origin: Russia and CEE	r	-.615**	1	.287*	-.193	-.074	.037
	Sig. (2-tailed)	.000		.024	.133	.569	.777
Gender (female)	r	.028	.287*	1	-.112	-.241	-.121
	Sig. (2-tailed)	.830	.024		.386	.060	.348
Age	r	-.054	-.193	-.112	1	-.284*	.420**
	Sig. (2-tailed)	.677	.133	.386		.025	.001
English native speaker	r	-.122	-.074	-.241	-.284*	1	-.003
	Sig. (2-tailed)	.346	.569	.060	.025		.984
Tenure (months)	r	.022	.037	-.121	.420**	-.003	1
	Sig. (2-tailed)	.864	.777	.348	.001	.984	

		Origin: Russia and CEE	Gender (female)	Age	English native speaker	Tenure (months)
Gender (female)	r	.088	1	-.026	.046	-.199
	Sig. (2-tailed)	.496		.839	.721	.121
Age	r	-.070	-.026	1	-.080	.534
	Sig. (2-tailed)	.590	.839		.534	.000
English native speaker	r	-.234	-.080	.046	1	.199
	Sig. (2-tailed)	.067	.534	.721		.121
Tenure (months)	r	.009	-.004	.661**	.199	1
	Sig. (2-tailed)	.946	.977	.000	.121	

*. Correlation is significant at the 0.05 level (2-tailed).
**. Correlation is significant at the 0.01 level (2-tailed).

Table 2: Means and Standard Deviations

	Mean	Std. Deviation	N
Scale 1	2.5860	1.26561	62
Scale 2	3.3065	1.59382	62
Scale 3	1.3750	.69061	62
Scale 4	4.2634	1.10988	62
CSE	3.5161	.52874	62
Altruism	2.9935	.58165	62
MSc IER&HRM / HRM	.4032	.49455	62
Any MSc in Politics, Development Studies or else	.2581	.44114	62
Any PhD programme	.0484	.21633	62
Any MSc in Economics	.1290	.33797	62
Origin Anglo-Saxon and Western Europe	.5645	.49987	62
Origin Asia	.2258	.42153	62
Origin Russia and CEE	.0968	.29806	62
Gender (female)	.5323	.50303	62
Age	24.5484	2.59051	62
English native speaker	.3387	.47713	62
Tenure (months)	24.1774	24.59143	62

References

Allen, P., Bennett, K. (2008): "SPSS for the Health and Behavioural Sciences". South Melbourne: Thomson

Anderson, R. (2007): "Thematic content analysis: Descriptive presentation of qualitative data". http://www.wellknowingconsulting.org/publications/pdfs/ThematicContentAnalysis.pdf ; retr. 21-07-2011

Aron, A., Aron, E. N. (1999): "Statistics for psychology". New Jersey: Prentice Hall

Bekkers, R. (2004): "Stability, reliability and validity of social value orientation". Working Paper, www.fss.uu.nl/soc/homes/bekkers/svo04.pdf ; retr. 19-11-2011

Bakker, M., Leenders, R.T.A.J., Gabbay, S.M., Kratzer, J., Van Engelen, J.M.L. (2006): "Is trust really social capital? Knowledge sharing in product development projects". *The Learning Organization* (13), 6: 594-605

Bargh, J.A., Chen, M., Burrows, L. (1996): "Automaticity of social behavior: Direct effects of trait construct and stereotype action on construct accessibility". *Journal of Personality and Social Psychology* (50): 869-878

Bargh, J.A., Gollwitzer, P., Lee-Chai, A., Barndollar, K., Trötschel, R. (2001): "The Automated Will: Nonconscious Activation and Pursuit of Behaviour Goals". *Journal of Personality and Social Psychology* (81), 6: 1014-1027

Bargh, J. A., Pietromonaco, P. (1982): "Automatic information processing and social perception: The influence of trait information presented outside of conscious awareness on impression formation". *Journal of Personality and Social Psychology* (43): 437-449

Blickle, G./Schlegel, F. (2006): "Some Personality Correlates of Business White-Collar Crime". *Applied Psychology: An international review* (55): 220-233

Bratton, V. K., Kacmar, K. M. (2004): "Extreme careerism: The dark side of impression management". In: Griffin, R., O'Leary-Kelly, A.M. (eds.): "The dark side of organizational behavior". San Francisco: Jossey-Bass: 291-308

Burks, S., Carpenter, J., Goette, L. (2005): "Performance pay and the erosion of worker cooperation: Field experimental evidence". *Department of Economics, Middlebury College Working Paper*

Carpenter, J., Seki, E. (2006): "Competitive Work Environments and Social Preferences: Field Experimental Evidence from a Japanese Fishing Community". *Contributions to Economic Analysis & Policy* (5), 2: article 2

Chen, K.-P. (2003): "Sabotage in Promotion Tournaments". *Journal of Law, Economics and Organizations* (19), 1: 119-140

Chen, S., Choi, C.J. (2005): "A Social Exchange Perspective on Business Ethics: An Application to Knowledge Exchange." *Journal of Business Ethics* (62): 1-11

Chiu, Y.-F., Spindel, B. (2009): "Running Head – Effect of Age and Gender on Ethical Decision Making, http://www.mikedillinger.com/SJSUpapers/ChiuSpindel2009_decisionMaking.pdf ; retr. 19-07-2011

Cortada, James W. (1998): "Rise of the Knowledge Worker". Butterworth-Heinemann: Boston

Darlington, R.B., Weinberg, S., Walberg, H. (1973): "Canonical variate analysis and related techniques". *Review of Educational Research* (43), 4: 433-454

Demerouti, E., Bakker, A. B., Nachreiner, F., Schaufeli, W. B. (2001): "The job demands-resources model of burnout". *Journal of Applied Psychology* (86): 499-512

Dijksterhuis, A., Spears, R., Postmes, T., Stapel, D. A., Koomen, W., van Knippenberg, A., Scheepers, D.(1998): "Seeing one thing and doing another: Contrast effects in automatic behavior". *Journal of Personality and Social Psychology* (75): 862–871

Drago, R., Garvey, G.T. (1998): "Incentives for helping on the job: Theory and evidence". *Journal of Labour Economics* 16: 1-25

Glass, R, Wood, W. (1996): "Situational Determinants of Software Piracy: An Equity Theory Perspective". *Journal of Business Ethics* (15): 1189-1198

Good, J.K. (1973): "Social Facilitation: Effects of Performance Anticipation, Evaluation and Response Competition on free associations". *Journal of Personality and Social Psychology* (28), 2: 270-275

Green, J., Stokey, N. (1983): "A Comparison of Tournaments and Contracts". *Journal of Political Economy:* 349-364

Green, S. (2007): "Lying, cheating and stealing: a moral theory of white collar crime". Oxford University Press: Oxford

Griffin, R. W., O'Leary-Kelly, A. M. (2004): "An introduction to the dark side". In: R. W. Griffin and A. M. O'Leary-Kelly (eds.): "The dark side of organizational behavior", San Francisco: Jossey-Bass: 1-19

Guy, M. (1990): "Ethical Decision Making in Everyday Work Situations". Quorum Books

Harrel-Cook, G., Ferris, G., Dulebohn, J. (1999): "Political behaviors as moderators of the perceptions of organizational politics – work outcomes relationships". *Journal of Organizational Behavior* (20): 1093-1105

Herr, P. M. (1986): „Consequences of priming: Judgment and behavior". *Journal of Personality and Social Psychology* (51): 1106–1115

Hertel, G., Kerr, N. L. (2001): "Priming in-group favoritism: The impact of normative scripts in the minimal group paradigm". *Journal of Experimental Social Psychology* (37): 316–324

Hertel, G., Fiedler, K. (1998): "Fair and dependent versus egoistic and free: Effects of semantic and evaluative priming on the 'Ring Measure of Social Values'." *European Journal of Social Psychology* (28): 49–70

Higgins, E. T., Rholes, W. J., & Jones, C. R. (1977): "Category accessibility and impression formation". *Journal of Experimental Social Psychology* (13): 141-154

Intellectual Property Office (2007): "Intellecutal property rights and entrepreneurship". *The Times Newspaper Limited and @MBA Publishing Ltd*, http://www.thetimes100.co.uk/downloads/ipo/ipo_13_full.pdf ; retr. 14-07-2011

Judge, T., Erez, A., Bono, J., Thoresen, C. (2003): "The Core Self-Evaluation Scale: Development of a Measure". *Personnel Psychology* (56): 303-331

Kay, A., Ross, L. (2003): "The perceptual push: The interplay of implicit cues and explicit situational construals on behavioural intentions in the Prisoner's Dilemma". *Journal of Experimental Social Psychology* (39): 634-643

Kay, A., Wheeler, C., Bargh, J.A., Ross, L. (2004): "Material priming: The influence of mundane physical objects on situational construal and competitive behavioral choice". *Organizational Behavior and Human Decision Processes (95)*: 83-96

Kleiman, T., Hassin, R.R. (2010): "Non-conscious goal conflicts". *Journal of Experimental Social Psychology* (47): 521-532

Krumrie, Matt (2010): "Office bandits: Are your co-workers stealing your ideas?". *Examiner.com*, http://www.examiner.com/workplace-in-minneapolis/office-bandits-are-your-co-workers-stealing-your-ideas ; retr. 16-07-2011

Langton, L., Piquero, A. (2007): "Can general strain theory explain white-collar crime? A preliminary investigation of the relationship between strain and select white-collar offenses". *Journal of Criminal Justice* (35): 1-15

Lauring, J., Selmer, J. (2010): "Multicultural organizations: Common language and group cohesiveness". International Journal of Cross Cultural Management (10), 3: 267-284

Lazear, E.P. (1989): "Pay Equality and Industrial Politics". *The Journal of Political Economy*, (97), 3: 561-580

Lazear, E.P., Gibbs, M. (2009): "Personnel Economics in Practice". New York: *Wiley*

Lazear, E.P., Rosen, S. (1981): "Rank-Order Tournaments as Optimum Labor Contracts". *The Journal of Political Economy* (89): 841-864

Lee, T.W. (1999): "Using qualitative methods in organizational research". Sage: Thousand Oaks

Marslen-Wilson, W., Komisarjevsky Tyler, L., Waksler, R. (1994): "Morphology and Meaning in the English Mental Lexicon". *Psychological Review* (101), 1: 3-33

Maxwell, S., Nye, P., Maxwell, N. (1999): "Less pain, some gain: The effects of priming fairness in price negotiations". *Psychology and Marketing* (16): 545–562

Patton, M. Q. (2002): "Qualitative research and evaluation methods". Sage: Thousand Oaks

Penner, L., Fritzsche, B.A., Craiger, P., Freifeld, T.S. (1995): "Measuring the prosocial personality". In: Butcher, J., Spielberger, C.D. (eds.): *Advances in personality assessment* (10). Hillsdale, New Jersey

Pidd, Helen (2011): "German defence minister resigns in PhD plagiarism row". *guardian.co.uk*, http://www.guardian.co.uk/world/2011/mar/01/german-defence-minister-resigns-plagiarism ; retr. 14-07-2011

Robinson, S., O'Leary-Kelly, A. (1998): "Monkey see, Monkey do: The influence of work groups on the antisocial behavior of employees". *Academy of Management Journal*, (41), 6: 658-672

Rosenfeld, P., Giacalione, R., and Riordan, C. (1995): "Impression Management in Organizations". Routledge: London

Salancik, G.J., Pfeffer, J. (1978): "A social information processing approach to job attitudes and task design". *Administrative Science Quarterly* (23): 224-253

Sawng, Y.W., Kim, S.H., Han, H.-S. (2006): "R&D group characteristics and knowledge management activities: A comparison between ventures and large firms". *International Journal of Technology Management* (35), 1-4: 241-261

Schettkat, R., Yocarini, L. (2003): "The Shift to Services: A Review of the Literature". *IZA Discussion Paper* (964), http://papers.ssrn.com/sol3/papers.cfm?abstract_id=487282 ; retr. 14-07-2011

Sims, R. (2003): "Ethics and Corporate Social Responsibility". Greenwood Publishing Group: Westport, Connecticut

Skarlicki, D. P., Folger, R. (2004): "Broadening our understanding of organizational retaliatory behavior". In: Griffin, R.W., O'Leary-Kelly, A.M. (eds.): "The Dark Side of Organizational Behavior", San Francisco: Jossey-Bass: 373-401

Smeesters, D., Warlop, L., Van Avermaet, E., Corneille, O., Yzerbyt, V. (2003): "Do Not Prime Hawks With Doves: The Interplay of Construct Activation and Consistency of Social Value Orientation on Cooperative Behaviour". http://www.psor.ucl.ac.be/personal/yzerbyt/Smeesters%20et%20al.%20JPSP%202003.pdf ; retr. 16-07-2011

Srull, T., Wyer, R. (1979): "The Role of Category Accessibility in the Interpretation of Information About Persons: Some Determinants and Implications". *Journal of Personality and Social Psychology* (37), 10: 1660 – 1672

Stapel, D., Koomen, W. (2005): "Competition, Cooperation, and the Effects of Others on Me". *Journal of Personality and Social Psychology* (88), 6: 1029-1038

Stapel, D., Koomen, W., Ruys, K. (2002): "The Effects of Diffuse and Distinct Affect". Journal of Personality and Social Psychology (83), 1: 60-74

Steinel, W., Utz, S., Koning, L. (2010): "The good, the bad and the ugly thing to do when sharing information: Revealing, concealing and lying depend on social motivation, distribution and importance of information. *Organizational Behavior and Human Decision Processes* 113: 85-96

Storbeck, J., Clore, G.L. (2008): "The affective regulation of cognitive priming". *Emotion* (8), 2: 208-215

Straughan, R. R.(1975): 'Hypothetical Moral Situations". *Journal of Moral Education*, (4), 3: 183 - 189

Streiner, D.L., Norman, G.R. (1989): "Health Measurement Scales: A Practical Guide to Their Development and Use". *Oxford Medical Publications*

Tversky, A., Kahneman, D. (1974): „Judgement under uncertainty: Heuristics and biases". *Science* (185),27: 1124-1131

Utz, S., Ouwerkerk, J.W., Van Lange, P.A.M. (2004): "What is smart in a social dilemma? Differential effects of priming competence on cooperation". *European Journal of Social Psychology* (34): 317-332

Wang, S., Noe, R. (2010): "Knowledge Sharing: A review and directions for future research". *Human Resource Management Review* 20: 115-131